New
Performance
Measures

The Master Management Series

William F. Christopher
Editor-in-Chief

4

New Performance Measures

Brian H. Maskell

PRODUCTIVITY PRESS

Portland, Oregon

Volume 4 of the *Management Master Series*.
William F. Christopher, Editor-in-Chief
Copyright © 1994 by Productivity Press, Inc.

Productivity Press
P.O. Box 13390
Portland OR 97213-0390
United States of America
Telephone: 503-235-0600
Telefax: 503-235-0909

ISBN: 1-56327-062-5

Book design by William Stanton
Composition by Rohani Design
Printed and bound by BookCrafters in the United States of America

Library of Congress Cataloging-in-Publication Data

Maskell, Brian H.
    New performance measures / Brian H. Maskell.
       p.   cm. -- (Management master series ; v. 4)
    Includes bibliographical references.
    ISBN 1-56327-062-5
    1. Industrial productivity--Measurement. 2. Labor productivity
--Measurement. 3. Performance. I. Title. II. Series.
HD56.25.M38   1994
658.5'1--dc20   94-27920
                                 CIP

98 97 96 95   10 9 8 7 6 5 4 3 2

—CONTENTS—

PUBLISHER'S MESSAGE

The *Management Master Series* was designed to discover and disseminate to you the world's best concepts, principles, and current practices in excellent management. We present this information in a concise and easy-to-use format to provide you with the tools and techniques you need to stay abreast of this rapidly accelerating world of ideas.

World class competitiveness requires managers today to be thoroughly informed about how and what other internationally successful managers are doing. What works? What doesn't? and Why?

Management is often considered a "neglected art." It is not possible to know how to manage before you are made a manager. But once you become a manager you are expected to know how to manage and to do it well, right from the start.

One result of this neglect in management training has been managers who rely on control rather than creativity. Certainly, managers in this century have shown a distinct neglect of workers as creative human beings. The idea that employees are an organization's most valuable asset is still very new. How managers can inspire and direct the creativity and intelligence of everyone involved in the work of an organization has only begun to emerge.

Perhaps if we consider management as a "science" the task of learning how to manage well will be easier. A scientist begins with an hypothesis and then runs experiments to observe whether the hypothesis is correct. Scientists depend on detailed notes about the experiment—the timing, the ingredients, the amounts—and carefully record all results as they test new hypotheses. Certain things come to be known by this method; for instance, that water always consists of one part oxygen and two parts hydrogen.

We as managers must learn from our experience and from the experience of others. The scientific approach provides a model for learning. Science begins with vision and desired outcomes, and achieves its purpose through observation, experiment, and analysis of precisely recorded results. And then what is newly discovered is shared so that each person's research will build on the work of others.

Our organizations, however, rarely provide the time for learning or experimentation. As a manager, you need information from those who have already experimented and learned and recorded their results. You need it in brief, clear, and detailed form so that you can apply it immediately.

It is our purpose to help you confront the difficult task of managing in these turbulent times. As the shape of leadership changes, the *Management Master Series* will continue to bring you the best learning available to support your own increasing artistry in the evolving science of management.

We at Productivity Press are grateful to William F. Christopher and our staff of editors who have searched out those masters with the knowledge, experience, and ability to write concisely and completely on excellence in management practice. We wish also to thank the individual volume authors; Cheryl Rosen and Diane Asay, project managers; Julie Zinkus, manuscript editor; Karen Jones, managing editor; Lisa Hoberg, Mary Junewick, and Julie Hankin, editorial support; Bill Stanton, design and production management; Susan Swanson, production coordination; Rohani Design, composition.

Norman Bodek
Publisher

1

WHY ARE NEW PERFORMANCE MEASURES NEEDED?

Companies need a new approach to performance measurement. As they strive toward world-class performance and face rapid change, the traditional methods of measurement become a hindrance. They no longer apply, they measure the wrong things, and they mislead people. Traditional performance measures cannot address the issues that are now important to world-class companies:

- quality
- productivity
- on-time delivery
- innovation
- teamwork
- flexibility
- short cycle times
- closeness to customers

CUSTOMERS EXPECT MORE

Times have changed and the focus of Western industry is changing. Our customers expect more of us. They expect 100 percent quality. They expect on-time delivery every time. They expect innovation, flexibility, and low prices. Our measurement systems must match these expectations.

1

CHANGES IN MANAGEMENT METHODS

Companies are making big changes in the way they manage people. Many companies are reducing their size. This often leads to reorganizing the company so it has fewer levels and fewer middle managers. Therefore, more authority and responsibility are delegated lower down in the organization (see Figure 1).

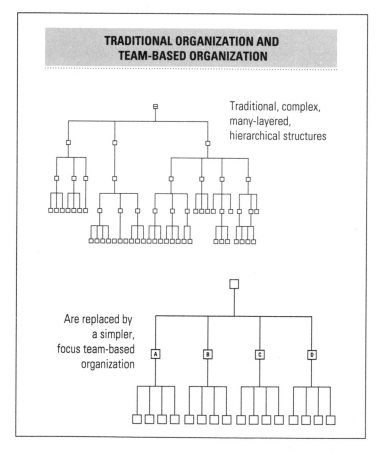

Figure 1. Traditional Organization and Team-based Organization

Social conditions also have changed. The old management methods that pit boss against worker don't work in the 1990s. The emphasis is on teamwork, leadership, and flexibility. And we need to measure these differently.

LONG-TERM GOALS—SHORT-TERM MEASURES

Many American managers focus on short-term results. Some appear to be interested only in quarterly financial results and the stock price. As a result companies have developed measurement systems that place undue emphasis on financial performance. Some experts think this is the main reason for America's manufacturing decline.[1] American companies never developed total quality management (TQM) and just-in-time manufacturing (JIT) because neither show short-term improvement in traditional financial measures.

MEASURES MUST LEAD PEOPLE IN THE RIGHT DIRECTION

The old performance measures make people do the wrong things. If quality is the goal, a labor variance report will not help. If close supplier relationships are important then purchase price variances (PPV) are misleading. A company that works for zero inventory does not need machine utilization measures. Companies must scrap traditional measures that represent the old way of thinking. We need new performance measures.

PROVIDING RESULTS TO KEEP THE ACCOUNTANTS HAPPY

When I was an inventory manager for Rank Xerox in Europe, I was responsible for spare parts inventory throughout 27 locations in 13 countries. The company measured my department by its adherence to the budgeted, monthly inventory levels for each country. For example, if Denmark was overstocked and Sweden was understocked, we raised orders to move materials from Denmark to Sweden. The Xerox cost accounting system was such that if an interplant order was raised the material was deemed to have arrived. Therefore, the company could manipulate inventory levels to meet the needs of the performance measurement system. We spent several days each month raising and later canceling these fictitious orders.

Was this good use of our time? Did this add value or serve the customers? Did we think about it? No. The inappropriate measurement method drove us to do ridiculous things instead of moving the company forward and improving customer service. And what made it worse was that we did not question it.

THE MOVE TOWARDS SIMPLICITY

Western companies have used computer systems to solve complex business problems. They developed MRP II—a complex system. The better Japanese companies, however, have gradually made their problems simpler. They developed *kanban*—a simple system. Simplicity is a primary key to world-class performance.

It is not easy to make things simple. It takes great skill, understanding, and attention to details to simplify business systems. It is far easier to create a highly complex model that few people use effectively and even fewer understand. This is true of the complex, financially based performance measurement systems we have developed over the years. Who really knows the *true significance* of an overhead absorption variance analysis?

WE NEED NEW PERFORMANCE MEASURES

We need new measures because the traditional ones are harmful and misleading. Our customers expect more from us. We must measure what our customers care about. The way we manage people is changing and measures need to change along with this. The move toward simplicity also applies to performance measures. We must line our performance measures up with the world-class goals of the organization. These goals include quality, flexibility, customer service and so forth. These issues must be the focus of the measures.

2

CHARACTERISTICS OF THE NEW PERFORMANCE MEASURES

Many companies have begun to use new performance measures that are in line with their world-class approach. Most of these performance measures are not new ideas. What is new: (1) The measures truly drive the business. (2) They replace traditional cost accounting. (3) They provide useful measures at all levels of the company.

Although every company applies these ideas differently, there are some common themes. Measures must:

- relate to business strategy

- be primarily nonfinancial

- vary between locations

- change over time

- be simple and easy to use

- provide fast feedback of information

- foster improvement rather than merely monitor performances

DIRECT RELATION TO BUSINESS STRATEGY

World-class companies have clear business strategies. These state the part each aspect of the business plays in the company's approach to its customers and market. Business strategies vary from one company to the next. Company leaders use business strategies to show what they want the company to be. For example, the strategy for a leading-edge company is quite different from one that makes sales through low prices and standard products.

The business strategy of a world-class manufacturer focuses on issues such as quality, reliability, short cycle times, flexibility, innovation, customer service, and environmental responsibility. Manufacturing strategy is one element of the company's business strategy, therefore performance measures must be in line with manufacturing strategy. New product development is another element of the business strategy. Sales and marketing is another element. Each needs performance measures that match the strategy.

There are three reasons for keeping performance measures in line with the business strategy.

- The first reason is obvious. A company needs to know how well it is performing. Choose a few measures the managers can use to assess progress.

- The second reason is that people focus on what you measure. If a company measures and reports someone's work, the person will want to improve his or her work. The choice of performance measures can steer company direction. The measures you choose show everyone the company's priorities.

- The third reason is that measures provide feedback to help people and teams to do their jobs and improve performance.

NONFINANCIAL MEASURES

Traditional companies focus on financial results. World-class companies stress nonfinancial measures. They do not use accounting reports to measure performance. The reports are not useful for daily control of the business. They are confusing and often misleading and they make people do the wrong things.

For performance measures to be relevant the company must express them in terms that directly relate to the business strategy. To disguise the results in financial terms is not helpful. Companies must measure results in terms that make direct sense to the people using them. For example, if the measures are in dollars, the operations people must translate them into something real. If you want to improve quality, measure quality—not cost of quality. If you are concerned about cycle time, measure cycle time—not labor-hours variances.

VARIATION AMONG LOCATIONS

Companies apply world-class manufacturing methods in many ways. Each plant is different: The products may differ; the customers may differ; the people may have different backgrounds. Plants in different countries are very different. A standard measurement method does not make sense.

Teams

Traditional companies use the same measures everywhere. They often pride themselves on being consistent. They often compare one plant to another. This is counterproductive. Teamwork is vital. Judging one against the other destroys the team. The real issue is improvement—not the actual value measured. People work in teams to improve the process. And teams do not work well together if they are rivals. Sharing information and ideas is positive. Judging one against another is not.

The Team Champion

To bring about major change you need a *champion*, a person who leads the team to success. Each plant may have a different champion. The champions most likely have different ideas and therefore, do the job differently. Do not hinder the champions by making them use standard measures. The standard measures will not apply to both plants. They would measure the wrong things and also frustrate the champions.

CHANGES OVER TIME

Measures need to change over time. Change is vital to a world-class company. All world-class companies value *continuous improvement*, a planned way for all employees to make their work better and better. Most changes are small, but when you put them together, they become a large step forward. When you introduce world-class methods, start with a big improvement followed by a continuous improvement program.

Continuous improvement is not a catchphrase. It is a way of life within world-class organizations. Continuous improvement means things change all the time. So performance measures must also change. When you start with world-class methods, some issues are more important than others. As time goes by, the important issues change. Measures must change to reflect this.

SIMPLICITY AND EASE OF USE

For performance measures to work people must understand them. Complex measures do not work. They confuse people and the measure itself becomes a problem. Don't use ratios. Don't use measures that combine many aspects into a single factor. Use plain and simple measures for the most important parts of the business. Measure each issue directly and present it well. People then find the results easy to use, and the measure is effective.

Performance measures in world-class companies are clear and direct. Often people make these measures on the spot using wall charts, and bulletin boards, graphs, signals, and computer screens. The best measures are the ones people make themselves. They understand them and trust the numbers.

A production plant, for example, can show measures throughout the day. They use boards, charts, and graphs located near the production cell. Direct reporting methods are good motivators because the shop-floor people can monitor their own progress. Everyone can see the results (see Figure 2).

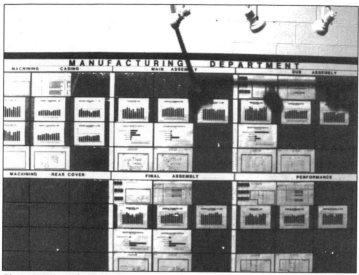

Photo courtesy of ZUA Auto Parts

Figure 2. Visual Reporting of Performance

Simple computer spreadsheets can also be helpful. Spreadsheet programs can work out the numbers, show the results, and also draw attractive graphs. The measures do not have to be pretty, but they must be clear, direct, and simple.

FAST FEEDBACK OF INFORMATION

Most companies get their measures monthly in the form of accounting reports that follow the accounting calendar. Often these reports are too late to be useful. And often people call time-wasting meetings to explain the variances. These meetings are to defend their actions—not to improve performance.

A world-class company fixes problems when they happen. It does not wait for the end of the month. For performance measures to improve performance the company needs the information fast. Action cannot wait until the middle of next month. Some information is needed on the spot. Quality, for example,

cannot wait. Other information is needed daily or twice daily, or perhaps, weekly. The feedback must match the need.

Continuous measurement, either manual or by automatic data capture gives fast feedback. Terminals nearby enable people to run reports when they need them. They do not need to wait for someone else's schedule. Fourth generation programming tools[2] let people get the data they need from the computer. They can get it when they need it and present it how they like it.

FOSTERING IMPROVEMENT RATHER THAN MERELY MONITORING IT

This characteristic of performance measurement for a world-class company concerns *motivation*. Although motivation is intangible, it is extremely important. A performance measurement system works only if the people using it find it helpful. It will not work if they feel they are being watched and judged.

Performance measures need to show clearly where improvement has been made and where more improvement is possible. They must do far more than monitor people's work. Traditional companies use measures to judge people. Often they use measures to blame people or to assess their prospects for pay and promotion. This creates fear, and fear stops people from getting better.

Measures must foster improvement. World-class companies use measures to help people improve. They want people to be creative, to try out new ideas, and to take risks.

The difference between judging people and helping them to improve may sound subtle, but it is the difference between success and failure. Many of the issues already discussed have an impact on how to use the measures to help people focus on improvement:

- on-time reports,

- easy-to-use charts and graphs,

- direct measurement, and

- measures that fit the company's business strategy.

3

EXAMPLES OF NEW PERFORMANCE MEASURES AT WORK

There are many approaches to performance measurement. The following examples show how some world-class companies measure performance. Every company must develop measures that are appropriate for their business. There is no standard set of measures that fit all organizations.

Companies often have too many measures. They assume that measuring many things creates more control. This is wrong. Too many measures create confusion and lack of focus. Pick out the six or eight measures that are sufficient to control your business and provide the balance of service, time, quality, and cost.

DELIVERY PERFORMANCE AND CUSTOMER SERVICE

Everybody has customers. They may be the people using the products or services the company makes, or they may be other people within the organization. The outside customer may pay the invoices, but even support departments (a technical library, for example) have customers within the organization that they need to satisfy. Measuring every customer's satisfaction is most important.

Measures of Customer Satisfaction

The best measures of customer satisfaction provide direct feedback from the customers. Direct feedback can either be through customer surveys or establishing automatic feedback.

Automatic feedback includes delivery reply cards with date and time stamps, questionnaires, or feedback from the carriers that deliver the products. A better form of automatic feedback is the use of electronic data interchange (EDI) from the customer confirming receipt of the product. Reply cards and questionnaires are limited because only a few customers return them. Once returned they must be entered into a tracking system. EDI receipt confirmation is more reliable and does not require additional data entry. The feedback information shows how good you are at delivering on time.

Obtaining Direct Feedback

Often direct feedback is difficult to obtain and measures such as on-time shipments are used to track customer service levels. These measures show the number of on-time deliveries and are usually presented as a graph (see Figure 3). An average company compares the date promised with the date shipped. A world-class company shows the date the customer requested against the date shipped. The customer need is what is important—not what was promised.

A company can obtain direct feedback by contacting the customer and asking questions. This information can be more helpful than that from reply cards and questionnaires because it shows not only statistics, but also how the customer feels about the company and the products. Companies often call every customer after each delivery of product or service. If there are many customers and many sales, then the company selects a sample of customers. Just a few questions are asked—five at the most. A questionnaire for marketing purposes may have many questions, but a performance measurement survey has just a few. The questions relate to on-time delivery, quality of the product, and overall satisfaction. The information obtained is presented using graphs and charts (see Figure 4).

Keep measures of customer service simple. Select one that addresses the customer's concerns, then drive the company's customer service objectives from this one measure. Do not use measures that combine several factors because these confuse people and do not lead to improvement.

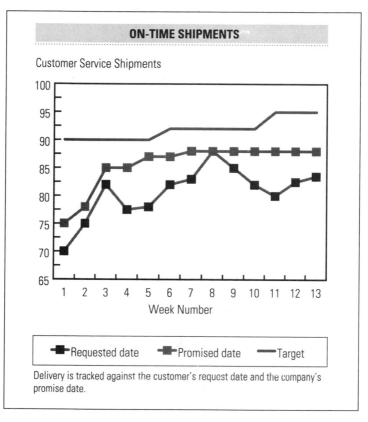

Figure 3. Example of On-Time Shipment Tracking

PROCESS TIME

All the jobs in a company are processes. These processes may span more than one department but they are, nevertheless, processes. In manufacturing, processes are easily defined and include making the product. In service and support areas the processes can be more difficult to define. Entering customer orders and meeting the customer needs is a process. Providing accounting information is a process. Designing new products or enhancing current products is a process. Any company can measure these process times.

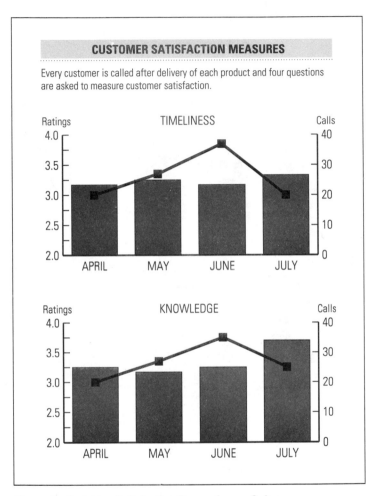

Figure 4. **Customer Satisfaction Survey from a Software Programming Organization**

Short Process Times

Short process times are essential for world-class companies. Short production process times result in low inventories because product can be made-to-order instead of made-to-stock.

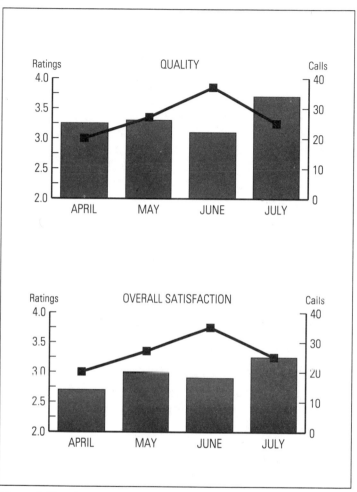

Figure 4. (Cont.)

Short process times provide low inventories because material flows through the production plant quickly and is not subject to queues or wait and move times. Short process times make a company more flexible to the needs of customers. Quick setups or changeovers are essential to short process times (see Figure 5).

CHANGEOVER TIMES – DOOR PANEL PRESS 3		
World Class	Today	Best Ever
12.30 minutes	*10.06 minutes*	9.42 minutes

Changeover time monitoring used by an innovative new American automobile manufacturer.

Figure 5. Changeover Monitor Display

Customer Service Time

World-class companies stress timely service to customers, both internal and external. A simple measure is customer service time. This is the time from receipt of the order to dispatch of the product or service (see Figure 6). It is a good measure of how quickly the customers are being served. Often it can be measured directly from the company's computer systems for order entry and shipping.

Measuring Process Times

If the information is already available in the computer system, process time measures are easily derived. Most world-class companies do not track a lot of detailed information about processes because this detailed tracking is wasteful. Do not introduce detailed tracking for performance measurement purposes only; it is non-value-added. Theoretical process times can be derived from production routings or process flow charts if these documents are accurate and up-to-date.

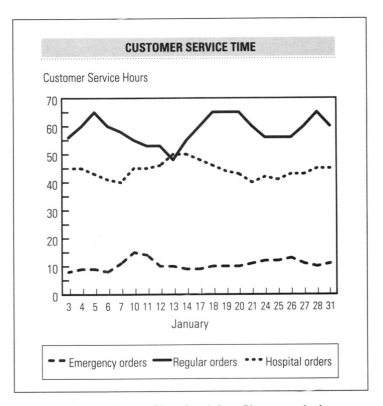

Figure 6. Customer Service Time Graph for a Pharmaceutical Equipment Distribution Company

Measuring by Sampling

Process times can be measured by sampling. If there are many jobs and it is not desirable to measure each one, then measure a sample. Every hour on the hour everyone stops and measures their process time, for example, measuring every 100th job in detail. Every tenth *kanban* card is a different color and has space for entering measurement information on the back of the card. This sample information is then gathered, analyzed, and reported in a graph or chart. Companies achieve radical reductions in process time as they introduce world-class methods. A Department of Defense repair operation reduced process time from 60 days to 8 days. A car seat manufacturer reduced customer lead times from 12 weeks to 90 minutes. The printed circuit board cell of an electronic equipment manufacturer reduced production cycle times from 1½ weeks to 1 day by introducing cellular manufacturing. These changes must be tracked and monitored.

Measuring Service and Support Processes

Similarly, companies can measure service and support processes. The time to create invoices measures the time between shipment and the invoice being mailed or sent through EDI. Other examples are the time to retrieve and deliver a reference book from the technical library; the time to complete a month-end financial close; and the time to resolve customer service calls. Figure 7 shows how a major software company measures customer support calls.

INNOVATION

In many industries innovation is a key to the future. Product life cycles are getting shorter and the ability to introduce new products, new services, and new procedures is vital. A world-class company stresses the need for every individual within the organization to be involved in improvement and innovation. It is not just new products that need innovation; so do new procedures and new services to customers.

Measuring Innovation

The method of measuring new product innovation varies according to the company and the market. An organization that introduces many new products can continuously measure the rate of new product introduction or the number of new products per month or year. Companies that have fewer new products can measure the time-to-market of product. The time-to-market is defined as the time from conception of the

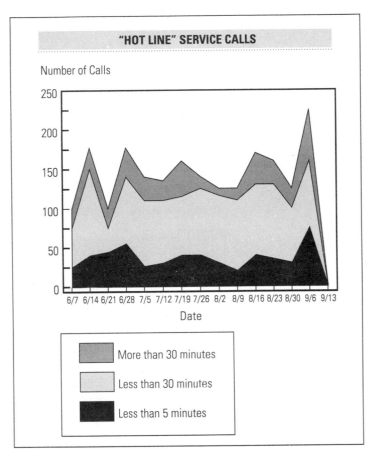

Figure 7. Measuring Customer Telephone Support Service

product to its introduction to the marketplace. One Honda plant in Japan regularly introduces a major product enhancement every month. They gear the production process and working hours around this need for new product introduction.

Employee Suggestion Systems

Another slant on innovation is the number of employee suggestions that are made and implemented. Many world-class companies have clearly defined employee suggestion systems. These methods keep careful track of who suggested what and how it was implemented. Advanced companies often record the changes after they are made because the people are empowered to make the changes on their own authority. A good measure of suggestions is the number of suggestions per person per year or month. Toyota Motor Company is recorded to have achieved around 35 suggestions per person. PSI Corporation in southern New Jersey is achieving 40 suggestions per person per year. Even though many of the suggestions are small, they add up to enormous improvement and very high employee involvement and commitment.

PRODUCTIVITY

Productivity is a measure of how good a company is at turning raw materials into products. It is a measure of wealth creation. In a service industry it is a measure of how effective the company is at providing the service with the minimum expenditure of resources.

Product and Service Measures

The best way to measure productivity in a company or a plant is to measure directly the number of products or services provided per person. Harley Davidson measures motorcycles per person per day. A pharmaceutical manufacturer measures tablets manufactured per person per day, irrespective of how these tablets are packaged. Figure 8 shows an example of productivity graphs.

It is important to define the people included in the productivity calculation. Ideally productivity measures should include everybody in the plant: the direct production people, the sales people, the engineers, the administrative people, and the managers. Often this is not possible because some of these "indirect" people may work on products related to more than one plant, or they may be located in another facility. It is

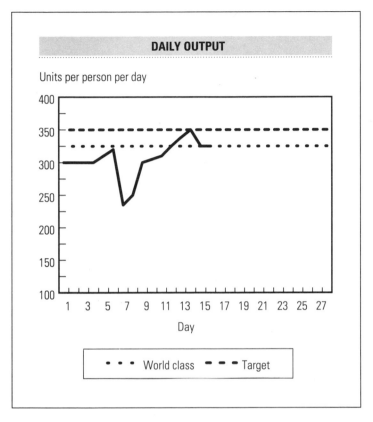

Figure 8. Productivity Measures

difficult to assign them to a specific product range. Most companies find that they can devise a sensible way of including a wide range of "direct" and "indirect" people into the calculation and making this a measure of the organization's overall effectiveness and productivity.

Financial Measures

Sometimes it is not possible to use a product or service measure because the company's product range includes widely different products, and the mix of products or services provided to customers changes from one week to the next or month to the next. This makes the measure invalid. When this happens it is necessary to move to a financial measure and use the value of product produced per person. It is important to understand the value and how it is calculated. It is easy for these measures to be misleading if the measure of value is not defined clearly and correctly. Most companies use the total standard cost of the products manufactured. This is reasonable, but you need to understand that the standard cost of a product includes a great deal of inefficiency and waste. The standard cost includes scrap, move time, wait time, batch sizes, and other wasteful activities. This measure can lead you in the wrong direction because the measure reduces as the standard cost is reduced. Therefore removing the waste from the process and reducing standard costs shows productivity going down—which it is not, of course.

When standard cost is inadequate for a productivity measure companies move to using list price, sales, or market value of the product. All of these approaches are fraught with problems of defining the *real* value of the product manufactured. It is for this reason that a nonfinancial measure should be found, if at all possible.

FLEXIBILITY

While the majority of Western manufacturers have been concentrating on improving quality, reducing costs, and (in many cases) implementing just-in-time manufacturing, the leading-edge Japanese companies have been looking further ahead. A survey done by the Boston Manufacturing Roundtable showed that leading Japanese manufacturers now foresee low price and flexibility as being the competitive edge issues. As Western manufacturers run to improve and move into high quality, high value-added, and just-in-time production, the leading competitors are also moving ahead in other areas.

Flexible Production

Flexibility is the ability to make today what the customers want today. Companies must be able to change product mix and volumes quickly, effectively, and economically as the customer needs change. Traditional companies provide for customer needs by maintaining finished goods inventories and making-to-stock. World-class companies build flexibility into their processes so they can make-to-order with very short lead times. Measures of flexibility are measures of the company's ability to meet this demand.

Flexible production is achieved through short cycle times, commonality, modular product design, a flexible work force, and having more capacity available than is typically required. Figure 9 shows measures of departmental cross-training use by a Florida fabrication company. To be considered a flexible manufacturer, you need to be able to make the product or provide the service more quickly than the customers expect. In many industries it is necessary to be able to receive an order today, make it tomorrow, and ship it in the afternoon—a genuinely 24-hour turnaround. A traditional company builds finished-goods inventory to achieve this level of customer service. A world-class company improves their production flexibility so that they can make today what the customers want today.

Measuring Flexibility

Many aspects of manufacturing have to be *right* for a company to achieve highly flexible production. Measuring flexibility involves measuring the aspects of the company's products and processes that create flexibility. Measurement of process times, discussed earlier, becomes a key measure for the flexible manufacturer.

To measure commonality of parts and processes, use the engineering data within the company's computer systems. To measure part commonality calculate the average number of

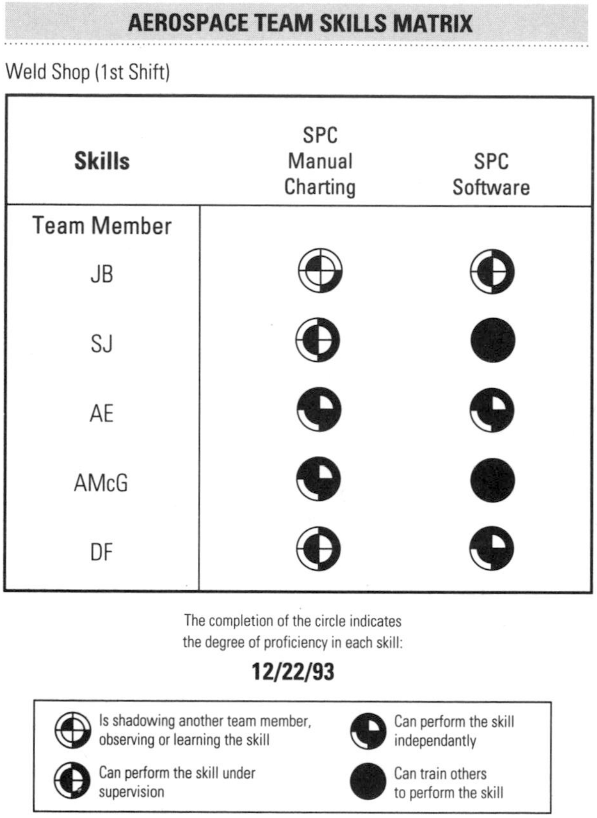

AEROSPACE TEAM SKILLS MATRIX

Weld Shop (1st Shift)

Skills	SPC Manual Charting	SPC Software
Team Member		
JB	◕	◐
SJ	◐	●
AE	◔	◔
AMcG	◔	●
DF	◐	◕

The completion of the circle indicates
the degree of proficiency in each skill:

12/22/93

◕	Is shadowing another team member, observing or learning the skill	◔	Can perform the skill independantly
◐	Can perform the skill under supervision	●	Can train others to perform the skill

One aspect of employee flexibility is the amount of cross-training within the cells. This simple, graphical chart shows the cross-training of employees and their ability to train others.

Source: METAL FAB Corporation. Used with permission.

Figure 9. Employee Cross-Training Chart

different products (or product families) that require a certain part. Most companies find it helpful to divide their component parts into three categories: unique parts (used only on one product or product family), common parts (used on many products or product families), and standard parts (used widely).

	PRODUCTION PART COMMONALITY		
PRODUCT LINE	NUMBER OF PARTS	CUM. NUMBER	UNIQUE
AS	1260	35215	293
AX	2598	33955	2433
AZ	243	31357	40
B1	1782	31114	1534
B2	232	29332	178
B10	8733	29100	8212
BC	9021	20367	5588
BZ	1221	11346	1091
MN	2890	10125	21
MM	2143	7435	670
SPARES	5271	5292	0
CONSUM	21	21	0

Figure 10. Part Commonality Analysis Used By An Electrical Equipment Manufacturer

Figure 10 shows an example of a commonality analysis. The company determines the precise definition of common, unique, and standard parts. Then they regularly measure the changing levels of commonality and plot them on a graph.

You also measure process commonality the same way, except you derive the information from the engineering information that relates to production processes. Then classify the processes according to their commonality of use. Finally, present charts that show the changing process commonality of the organization.

Measuring Modularity

Modular product design greatly enhances flexibility. If a company manufactures the finished product by configuring a relatively small number of major subassemblies, then final assembly can be very flexible. If they determine specific finished product in the early stages of manufacture (fabrication, for example), then the production process is much less flexible. Building modularity into the design of the product is a major objective for many world-class companies. The objective is to provide maximum variety for the customers while maintaining minimum variety within the production process. This is an art rather than a science and requires considerable engineering skill and judgment.

Measuring of modularity is difficult because the definition of modularity varies so much from one company to another. One approach is to use the *position of variability*. This is the point in the production process or the bill of materials where the finished product is differentiated. After this point it is not possible to change the finished product being manufactured. Measure it by calculating the average position of variability for the products and plotting this over time as the modularity is engineered into the product families.

QUALITY

To say that quality is an important aspect of world-class manufacturing is an understatement. Some companies would say that quality *is* world-class manufacturing—that everything else stems from a quality approach. The success of many major Japanese companies truly is rooted in their longterm commitment to the improvement of quality.

Building Quality into the Production Process

Quality is manufactured into a product. Traditional companies attempt to inspect poor quality out of a product. This is never successful in the long term and is the most expensive way of providing quality products to customers. To design quality into the product, a company must engineer the product and the production process so that it can achieve a high quality product. Vendor quality is also an important aspect. It is not possible to make consistently high-quality products when the raw materials and components from vendors are not good.

Building quality into the production process also requires sound management of the production floor.

- The physical layout of the shop floor is important. Cellular manufacturing lends itself to quality because the people who use the output from one stage of manufacture are adjacent to the people who produce it. This way they can immediately identify and resolve problems.

- Small batch sizes create high quality because problems are identified quickly and affect only a small quantity—one batch at most.

- Good housekeeping on the shop floor is essential for high quality production. The so-called 5 S approach includes *seiri* (proper arrangement), *seiton* (orderliness), *seiso* (cleanliness), *seiketsu* (cleanup), *shitsuke* (discipline). These five issues add up to a production floor that is tidy, focused, and productive.

- Statistical process control (SPC) is an important tool for creating quality in the production process. SPC is a simple, graphic method of giving the production operators the opportunity to monitor the process continuously and to ensure that the process is under control. SPC highlights variability in the production process. This can reveal causes of variability so they can be eliminated.

- Quality circles or participation teams are an essential element of building quality into the production process. Traditional companies attempt to improve quality by having industrial engineers work on solving problems. World-class companies improve quality by giving authority and responsibility for quality to the people on the shop floor who make the product, or the people in the office who serve the customers. Teams track down the true causes of problems and have the authority to eliminate those causes. Often companies use SPC to determine if the process is under control and as the starting point for investigating quality problems.

Measuring Quality

Measuring quality can start with the suppliers. Measuring the quality of incoming material enables you to create reports of vendor quality. However, a world-class company wants to avoid a lot of in-coming inspection of components and raw material because this is a non-value-added activity. The objective is to certify individual suppliers to provide components and raw materials that are up to standard and on time.

CERTIFYING SUPPLIERS

Certification is a long process of developing close, mutually beneficial relationships with a small number of suppliers. It involves single-sourcing of materials and components to the certified suppliers and ensuring that the suppliers are building quality into their production processes instead of trying to inspect poor quality out of the product. A world-class manufacturer aims to have certified vendors supply the vast majority of components and materials on a just-in-time basis. The objective is to avoid incoming inspection on these materials. Measures of supplier quality start off as reject rate based on incoming inspection, then move into measuring the amount of material received from certified suppliers.

REJECT RATE

Production quality is almost always measured in terms of rejects per thousand or rejects per million items (see Figure 11). This is a straightforward, easy to understand method of measuring quality. Another approach measures the number of processes that use statistical process control (SPC) and the

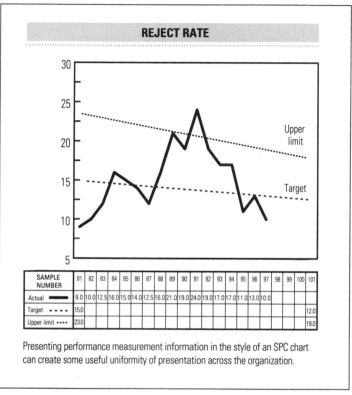

REJECT RATE

SAMPLE NUMBER	81	82	83	84	85	86	87	88	89	90	91	92	93	94	95	96	97	98	99	100	101
Actual ▬▬	9.0	10.0	12.5	16.0	15.0	14.0	12.5	16.0	21.0	19.0	24.0	19.0	17.0	17.0	11.0	13.0	10.0				
Target ----	15.0																				12.0
Upper limit ····	23.0																				19.0

Presenting performance measurement information in the style of an SPC chart can create some useful uniformity of presentation across the organization.

Figure 11. Reject Rate Chart

number of those processes that are "under control." This assumes that the majority of the production processes are appropriate for SPC and that using SPC creates improvement within the production process.

CUSTOMER SATISFACTION

Customer satisfaction is another good measure of quality. It measures not only the quality of the product but the quality of the service the customer is receiving. Customer satisfaction is best measured by direct feedback from customer surveys. A company with many customers may need to survey a sample number, others can survey all the customers. The key to surveys is to keep them brief and focused, and to contact the right people within the company. Some companies use "snake charts" (see Figure 12) because they show not only the customers' opinions of the service given but also the importance they place on each aspect of the service. We may do a great job and score very highly on issues the customers consider unimportant, while scoring poorly on aspects the customers consider to be of higher significance. Figure 13 shows an innovative, visual approach to measuring defects reported by customers.

Other quality issues to measure involve the accuracy of information within the computer system. You cannot be a world-class manufacturer and maintain high levels of product

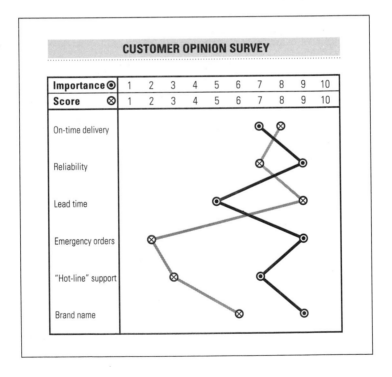

Figure 12. Customer Service Snake Chart

Products rejected by customers are displayed by year and department responsible for the defect. Photo courtesy of ZUA Auto Parts.

Figure 13. A Simple and Visual Quality Measure

quality if your information is poor. Primary issues are inventory accuracy, forecast accuracy, bill of materials accuracy, and production routing accuracy.

INVENTORY ACCURACY

Many companies measure inventory accuracy through their cycle counting program. Although cycle counting is a better approach than the old-fashioned annual physical inventory, it is still a wasteful activity. Eliminate it once inventory is under control. If you use cycle counting now, then also use it to report inventory accuracy. If you are not using cycle counting, then implement a simple method for the stockroom people to record the stock figures in the computer and the actual amounts available. (Typically these are identified by physical shortages.) Record the inventory accuracy on a hand-drawn chart in the stockroom (see Figure 14).

BILL OF MATERIAL ACCURACY AND ROUTING ACCURACY

Bill of material accuracy and routing accuracy is best measured by the people on the shop floor who use the information. Create a simple mechanism that the shop floor operators can use to signal when they find a BOM (bill of material) or routing

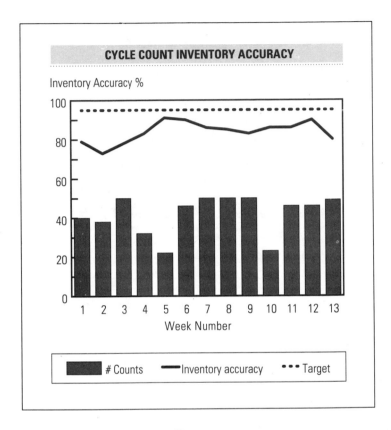

Figure 14. Inventory Accuracy Chart

inaccuracy. They can also use this mechanism to resolve the accuracy problem. The best way to solve accuracy problems is to give the shop floor operators—the people who use the information—the authority to change the BOMs and routings. If they require engineering assistance to do this, then provide them with quick access to the appropriate engineers.

FORECAST ACCURACY

Forecast accuracy is vital to the flexible, short lead-time manufacturer. The best way to make forecasts accurate is to make the production cycle time short so you can make to order. That way you would not need to have forecasts at all. In reality, most companies need forecasts for master production scheduling even if their final assembly is entirely make-to-order. The accuracy of these forecasts is a key issue and often a cause of conflict within the organization. The sales and marketing people attempt to predict sales while the production people attempt to plan production and purchase long lead time components.

Measuring forecast accuracy is difficult because it requires clear definition of the forecast. A general rule of thumb is to measure forecast accuracy for finished product SKUs (stock-keeping units) (not by product family and not by sales amount) as the actual sales quantity compared to the forecast that was one lead time prior to shipment. Present the information as a graph and split the forecast accuracy by product families to distinguish newer products, which are harder to forecast, from established product lines.

FINANCIAL PERFORMANCE MEASURES

While nonfinancial performance measures are better than financial measures, there are some legitimate reasons to use financial measures. The primary reason for using a financial measure is to establish a *common denominator* to consolidate dissimilar information on a single report.

There are two cautions when using financial performance measures:

- Define financial measures very carefully. Very often companies use standard costs, sales figures, market value, and the like in ways that can be quite misleading.

- Using financial reports to compare plants, locations, and departments is not compatible with a world-class approach, which emphasizes teamwork and continuous improvement. Teamwork breaks down when companies make judgmental comparisons between plants or departments. Similarly, the real issue is not the actual value of the measure, but the way it changes over time. To compare dissimilar plants or locations is not helpful and damages the company's world-class objectives. If you use financial measures to compare different parts of your company, stop and develop nonfinancial measures that are appropriate to the different needs of each location.

Scrap Rate

A common financial performance measure is scrap rate. Scrap occurs throughout the production processes at all levels and in all departments. It is often necessary to consolidate the amount of product scrapped throughout the process. World-class companies often focus very clearly on scrap because it is a measure of production quality. Reporting the amount of material scrapped each day is a good measure of how the quality of the production processes is changing. Figure 15 shows an example of scrap reporting.

Inventory Turns

Inventory turns is another measure that is very common within world-class companies. While this is not presented in financial terms the information is usually derived from financial information, often directly from the balance sheet and P&L. At first, a company can report stock turns separately for raw material, work-in-process, and finished products. Later, when world-class manufacturing methods begin to change the production process, the company shows the stock turns information for raw materials and finished products only. Later, as they move toward a *four wall* inventory, which does not mark or record the distinction between different kinds of stock, the company will report stock turns as a single figure.

Many companies report stock turns differently for different kinds of inventory. Many use *ABC analysis*, which splits the parts and raw material into categories based on use of the item. Clearly a fast-moving, high-value item is handled differently from a slow-moving, low-cost item. Reporting stock turns by ABC code enables companies to monitor these differences.

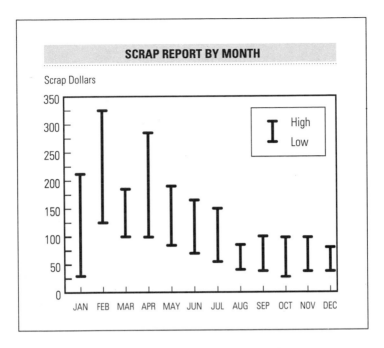

Figure 15. Scrap Reporting Using "Upper & Lower" Charts

Value-Added Analysis

Value-added analysis (VAA) is a powerful tool for creating improvement within a company. Basically, VAA examines the company's processes and determines which activities add value to the product or service from the *customer's point of view* and which are support activities. The ratio of value-added to nonvalue-added activities is a crucial measure of the company's productivity and effectiveness.

There is no such thing as a correct value-added ratio for a company because so much depends upon the way they define the activities. The trend, however, must aim to eliminate nonvalue-added, wasteful activities. Value-added analysis is a spin-off from activity-based costing. It is a good way for accounting to have a positive impact on the production or service processes of the company. Alternatively, a company can derive the value-added ratio of the production processes themselves from the production routings. If the routings are accurate, then the company can designate each step in the process as value-added or nonvalue-added and produce a simple report showing how much of the production activity during the previous period is value-added. Similarly, they can run these routings against the master production schedule and calculate future value-added amounts.

Product Cost

The cost of a product can also be an important measure. If a company makes similar products, the cost of the average product is a good measure of overall productivity. The cost of the product must be clearly understood. Ideally, take the total cost of running the plant (direct costs, indirect costs, expenses, etc.) and divide it by the total quantity of product produced to determine the average cost of products by the week, month, or year. You can also present this in a month-to-date and year-to-date format.

If determining the product costs is complicated, and if the costs include allocation of overhead costs using overhead allocation percentages, this measure ceases to be useful because the costs are not clearly understandable. If materials costs are volatile or if there are transfer cost issues, then the cost measure can include just the labor costs and total overhead costs and ignore material costs. The measure then becomes the *conversion cost* or *cost of adding value* per unit of production. Similarly *overhead efficiency* measures track only the overhead costs and do not account for materials or any direct labor costs. The overhead costs per unit of production can be a useful measure of the efficiency of the organization.

SOCIAL ISSUES

Everybody recognizes that the issues of teamwork, morale, leadership, and participation are crucial to a world-class company. Yet these issues are difficult to measure. Traditional measures make no attempt to address these issues, but focus only on the bottom line. While these issues are difficult to measure and are substantially intangible, companies can use a number of approaches to try to gauge their success in these areas.

Measuring Morale and Teamwork

Companies often measure morale and teamwork using the time-honored negative measures of employee turnover, productive days lost through absenteeism, and so forth. You can derive more positive measures of morale and teamwork from direct measures of the people's involvement in participatory activities, such as:

- the percentage of people in participatory teams (providing these teams are voluntary)

- the number of suggestions per person

- the number of suggestions implemented

- the amount of education or training classes taken per person

- the average number of certified skills per person within the plant or office.

Measuring Leadership

Leadership can be measured using personnel surveys and work environment measures. These measures vary from the highly complex sociological surveys to straight-forward questionnaires. One of the complex measures is the Stanford Work Environment Scale, which uses three questionnaires to measure such issues as involvement, peer cohesion, autonomy, and so forth. The three questionnaires look for the employees' assessment of the ideal company, what they expect from their company, and what they consider to be the actual situation. These surveys are then analyzed to determine the quality of the leadership and management within the organization. These kinds of surveys provide detailed and sociologically viable results. They have been culturally translated so that they apply in many different countries. They are, however, difficult to administer, and people often find the forms intimidating.

Such organizations as Kodak and the Federal Census Bureau have devised simpler forms. These forms ask straightforward questions like "Does your manager provide you with adequate training?" and "Do you feel part of a team in your department?". Typically, you administer two questionnaires, one dealing with expectations and the other with the reality. Analyzing and graphing the results shows the degree to which people within the organization feel motivated and involved.

Measuring Safety and the Environment

World-class companies tend to be very concerned about safety and environmental issues. They often establish safety and environmental audits within the organization. These audits are typically more stringent than government regulations and are conducted on a regular basis throughout the organization. Reports of the results show the degree to which each department or area adheres to the company's safety and environmental code.

4

IMPLEMENTING NEW PERFORMANCE MEASUREMENT

A new measurement system is a major change. A company must introduce it as it would any other major change—with great care. Do not be tempted to do a "quick and dirty" implementation. Changing measures changes the way people work. What you measure is what you get. New measures focus attention on those issues you choose to measure.[3]

Before you start looking for new ways to measure you need to ask yourself some tough questions.

IS THIS DECISION GOOD FOR MY ORGANIZATION?

A new approach to measurement will not work if the company continues to be controlled by traditional methods. The measurement system must fit with the company's world-class goals.

Take a hard look at your organization. Ask questions like:

- Are we serious about being a world-class company?

- Do we have real plans to make quality "Job One"?

- Will we stop using the current measurement system?

- What problems do we have with our current measurement system?

- How do these problems manifest?

- What do we want to accomplish by implementing a new approach to performance measurement?

- How will this new approach affect our customers, our production and distribution people, our clerical and support staff, product design and engineering people, senior managers, etc.?

- What benefits do we expect from the new performance measurement system?

HOW BIG A CHANGE IS THIS FOR MY ORGANIZATION?

Some companies already have good measurement systems. You may want to change the measures, focus them, or extend them. But these changes are not radical. Other companies have run for years on the old management accounting measures. New measures will bring significant, even radical, change. The bigger the change the more carefully you must plan it. Ask questions like these:

- Do we have a clear strategy for manufacturing, distribution, or service?

- Are our current measures well integrated with our strategies?

- Are we "run by the numbers" or do we have good nonfinancial measures already?

- Is there good communication flow within the company?

- Do we have simple charts and graphs that show our results?

- Are our current measures timely?

- Are the current measures flexible? Do they vary from one plant or location to another?

- Do we punish people or teams for bad results, or do we use measures to create improvement?

GETTING READY TO CHANGE PERFORMANCE MEASURES

MAKE A TEAM

A team of people from the affected operational areas should set up the new performance measurement system. The team must also include accountants, engineers, sales people, and managers. Bring together a varied team, one that represents all aspects of the business. If you need some guidance—add an outside consultant to the team.

TRAIN THE TEAM

Cross-functional teams need clear goals. They must understand their objectives. Set up a training class in performance measurement. Some people will need more training than others. Discuss the ideas and objectives fully. Make sure everyone is "on the team." If required, train the people in team skills, conflict resolution, team dynamics, and visual problem solving methods.

UNDERSTAND THE POLITICS

Any new system has enemies. New systems also have supporters. Make a list of who will support and who will detract. Understand that no one likes change. Everyone resists change unless they see a reason for it. Understand what people gain and lose by the new system. Try to "sell" the detractors on the new system. Obtain help from the supporters. Do not expect everything to go smoothly. Recognize that change is difficult for people, and help them through it.

MAKE A COMMUNICATIONS PLAN

Communication can resolve most objections. If your team works on its own, people will be suspicious. If you keep people informed, they will understand and support you. The communication plan may be as simple as circulating meeting minutes. It could also be a newsletter or a notice board with information about the project. Work with the union people—if you have them.

MAKE A PROJECT PLAN

Just like any other major project, you need a plan. Set dates, assign tasks, and schedule activities.

STEPS TO IMPLEMENTING
NEW PERFORMANCE MEASUREMENT

There are six steps to a new approach to performance measurement:

1. Write a strategy.

2. List the key strategic issues.

3. Validate the strategic issues.

4. Develop the measures.

5. Use the measures in a "pilot" area.

6. Expand the measures to the whole plant or company.

Step 1: Write a Strategy

Most companies have a clear business plan. All companies have strategies. Often these strategies are not written down or even thought out. Strategies show how the company will achieve the business plan. For example, a manufacturer has a manufacturing strategy; all companies have sales and marketing strategies (see Figure 16). Most companies have a product development strategy, a customer service strategy, and a financial plan.

MANUFACTURING STRATEGY

A manufacturing strategy guides you toward the kind of manufacturer you want to be: high-volume, low-price maker of standard products, an innovative, custom manufacturer, or a responsive, just-in-time supplier. The strategy also shows how you serve your customers, and how you treat your people. It may also address health, safety, and environmental issues.

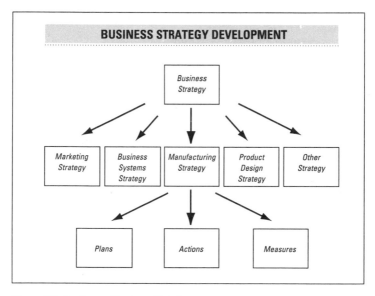

Figure 16. Business Strategy Development

MARKETING STRATEGY

A marketing strategy describes how to market and sell your products or services and your relationship to your customers. It may also describe the relationship with your competitors. Some strategy choices:

- a direct sales force
- franchises
- distributors
- focused retail outlets or discount stores
- a "technical sell," engineer to engineer
- a battery of telemarketers cold-calling to people's homes
- a full-service supplier or a niche company

WRITING

A strategy should be brief—two or three paragraphs at the most. The strategy should be clear. Anyone reading it must be able to understand it. A strategy is *not* a vision statement. It does not present a philosophy. A strategy presents a clear and practical approach to your business.

The team should review the company's existing written strategies. If they are good, use them. If no written strategy exists, write one and review it with people in the company. Everyone needs to agree that the strategy makes sense, including senior managers, middle managers, and the people doing the real work of serving the customers.

Do not underestimate the importance of having a well-written strategy. Make sure everyone buys into it. The performance measurement system will be built upon this strategy. It must be an accurate reflection of the company that everyone understands. Spend time to get it right.

Step 2: List the Key Strategic Areas

Once the team writes the strategy, they can define the *key strategic areas*. These are the detailed methods the company uses to be successful. The key strategic areas are the actions the company takes to make the strategy real. The strategy is the path to success. The key strategic areas are the stepping stones on the path.

Make a list of what must be done to put the strategy into action. Review the items carefully with the people responsible for making things happen. Include the managers, the people on the shop floor, the people in the office, and people in the field.

Step 3: Validate the Key Strategic Areas

It is easy to have great ideas. It is easy to have a grand strategy. But a strategy becomes reality only when you put it into action. Examine the key strategic areas carefully. Make a list of the actions the company has taken to make each strategic area real.

Many companies pay "lip service" to such issues as serving the customer, providing high quality, and achieving world-class service. Check that you really mean business—that you are really taking steps to bring the strategy to life. Only tangible actions make a strategy real.

Step 4: Develop the Measures

Once everyone understands and validates the strategy, you are ready to develop new measures. Do not create measures prematurely. Make sure the strategy and key areas are well understood first.

Every measure must meet the seven criteria described in Section 2. Link each measure to a key strategic area. Think about the format for reporting the measure. Consider these questions seriously:

- Where will the data come from?

- How easy is it to gather the data?

- What makes this a good measure?

- What are the weaknesses of the measure?

- Can the measure be consolidated across departments or cells?

REPORTING MEASURES

The best measures are reported directly by the people using them. The best measures use data that is already available for other reasons. Make that a rule in your company. Gathering more data can be wasteful.

The best measures are presented graphically. Pictures are better than words and numbers. Plan the format carefully. Can the people who use the measures draw their own charts? Are the measures flexible enough to meet the needs of each cell or department? Do you need different measures for each cell or department?

Some companies focus on presentation. They specify how to present measures but not how to calculate them. For example, to report quality, throughput time, cost, and customer service, every department must show their results on four graphs presented on a single sheet of paper. Each cell or department devises their own measures but they present them in the same format.

If each area or department devises their own measures, it is difficult to consolidate measures across more than one department. Gathering and reporting data manually also makes consolidation difficult. If consolidation is important in your company, it is best to gather and report the data through a computer system.

Step 5: Pilot the New Performance Measures

As with most significant changes, try the measure out before committing to it. Start using the new performance measures in a *pilot* area of the plant or company. Select a self-contained part of the business, develop the measures, and put them into p. actice. The pilot will reveal any shortcomings in the measures. It will also be a method of showing how a new approach to measurement is helpful.

Step 6: Expand the Measures to the Whole Plant or Company

Once the pilot has shown that the new measures work well, expand them to the entire plant. This requires abandoning the old measures. This is where the "rubber meets the road." It takes courage to abandon the old measures, but it must be done. You cannot have two performance measurement systems running at the same time.

Make sure the people who use the new measures are trained. It is important to show people why the new measures are better. If the new measures present a bigger challenge—they need more education. Have the team members available for informal training and encouragement.

5

A SPUR TO ACTION

Traditional approaches to performance measurement are harmful to organizations moving into the new and competitive world of the '90s and beyond. Our customers expect more of us and we must measure what matters to the customer. Teamwork, employee involvement, and partnership totally change the relationships within companies and the measures must reflect these changes.

There is no formula for developing relevant and meaningful measures, but there are principles to apply; Figure 17 recaps these criteria. The measures must match the company's strategic direction and should primarily be nonfinancial measures. The measures must be considerably flexible so they can vary from one location, product family, or market segment to another. They must also be able to change readily as the company's situation changes. Measures must be timely and easy to

---

New performance measures must:
- relate directly to business strategy
- be primarily nonfinancial
- vary between plants & locations
- change over time
- be simple and easy-to-use
- provide fast feedback
- foster improvement rather than just monitor performance

Figure 17. Criteria for a New Performance Measurement Approach

use if they are to be effective as motivators and aids to problem resolution. A company must use them to solve problems and instigate improvement instead of to reward and punish. World-class companies use measures to foster improvement as well as measure performance. This is a significant change in thinking for Western companies.

To a large extent, what you measure is what you get. The characteristics of the performance measurement system are useful indicators of a company's style and direction. Companies striving for excellence, quality, delighted customers, and long-term viability in the twenty-first century focus their measures on these issues and implement them through teamwork and employee involvement.

This approach is not easy. Change is always painful. Changing a measurement system cuts to the core of a company's culture. The future is always unclear, but we do know that agile and innovative organizations that are prepared to instigate and welcome change will win the competitive challenge. In the elegant words of Dr. W. Edwards Deming, "take action now to accomplish transformation." In the less elegant words of a factory foreman I know well, "If we don't get off our butts, someone else will kick our butts."

NOTES

1. H. Thomas Johnson. *Relevance Regained.* New York: Free Press, 1992.

2. Brian Maskell. *Software and the Agile Manufacturer.* Portland, Ore.: Productivity Press, 1994.

3. The author has written a workbook that contains a series of forms designed to guide a person or project team through the process of implementing a new approach to performance measurement. The worksheets address such issues as project team selection, the development of a strategy and key strategic areas, design of performance measures, the suitability of new performance measures to your company, and writing a project plan. *Performance Measurement Workbook*, Brian Maskell Associates Inc., Suite 110, 100 Springdale Road, Cherry Hill, NJ 08003.

ABOUT THE AUTHOR

Brian H. Maskell, president of Brian Maskell Associates, Inc., has more than 20 years' experience in manufacturing and distribution, in management positions ranging from shop-floor store supervisor for an electronics company to manager of European inventories for Xerox Corporation to vice president of product development and customer service for Unitronix Corporation. Over the past 10 years, his consulting practice has taken him to a wide variety of manufacturers in the United States, England, and Europe, where he assisted in the implementation of advanced manufacturing techniques including just-in-time, TQM, world-class performance measurement, and advanced management accounting.

A sought-after speaker and presenter, Mr. Maskell regularly presents papers at national and international conferences and presents public seminars in the U.S. and abroad on advanced manufacturing and management accounting approaches. He is the author of three books, including *Performance Measurement for World-Class Manufacturing* (Productivity Press, 1991), and *Software and the Agile Manufacturer* (Productivity Press, 1994).

The Management Master Series

The *Management Master Series* offers business managers leading-edge information on the best contemporary management practices. Written by highly respected authorities, each short "briefcase book" addresses a specific topic in a concise, to-the-point presentation, using both text and illustrations. These are ideal books for busy managers who want to get the whole message quickly.

Set 1 — Great Management Ideas

1. *Management Alert: Don't Reform—Transform!*
   Michael J. Kami

   Transform your corporation: adapt faster, be more productive, perform better.

2. *Vision, Mission, Total Quality: Leadership Tools for Turbulent Times*
   William F. Christopher
   Build your vision and mission to achieve world class goals.

3. *The Power of Strategic Partnering*
   Eberhard E. Scheuing
   Take advantage of the strengths in your customer-supplier chain.

4. *New Performance Measures*
   Brian H. Maskell
   Measure service, quality, and flexibility with methods that address your customers' needs.

5. *Motivating Superior Performance*
   Saul W. Gellerman
   Use these key factors—nonmonetary as well as monetary—to improve employee performance.

6. *Doing and Rewarding: Inside a High-Performance Organization*
   Carl G. Thor
   Design systems to reward superior performance and encourage productivity.

Set 2 — Total Quality

7. *The 16-Point Strategy for Productivity and Total Quality*
   William F. Christopher and Carl G. Thor

   Essential points you need to know to improve the performance of your organization.

8. *The TQM Paradigm: Key Ideas That Make It Work*
   Derm Barrett

   Get a firm grasp of the world-changing ideas behind the Total Quality movement.

9. *Process Management: A Systems Approach to Total Quality*
   Eugene H. Melan

   Learn how a business process orientation will clarify and streamline your organization's capabilities.

10. *Practical Benchmarking for Mutual Improvement*
    Carl G. Thor

    Discover a down-to-earth approach to benchmarking and building useful partnerships for quality.

11. *Mistake-Proofing: Designing Errors Out*
    Richard B. Chase and Douglas M. Stewart

    Learn how to eliminate errors and defects at the source with inexpensive poka-yoke devices and staff creativity.

12. *Communicating, Training, and Developing for Quality Performance*
    Saul W. Gellerman

    Gain quick expertise in communication and employee development basics.

These books are sold in sets. Each set is $85.00 plus $5.00 shipping and handling. Future sets will cover such topics as Customer Service, Leadership, and Innovation. For complete details, call 800-394-6868 or fax 800-394-6286.

BOOKS FROM PRODUCTIVITY PRESS

Productivity Press provides individuals and companies with materials they need to achieve excellence in quality, productivity and the creative involvement of all employees. Through sets of learning tools and techniques, Productivity supports continuous improvement as a vision, and as a strategy. Many of our leading-edge products are direct source materials translated into English for the first time from industrial leaders around the world. Call toll-free 1-800-394-6868 for our free catalog.

Software and the Agile Manufacturer:
Computer Systems and World Class Manufacturing
Brian Maskell

The term "agile manufacturing" describes responsive, flexible manufacturing that can deliver better products, faster, at lower cost. This book is the first to address the critical question of how computerization can aid the transition. It shows how computer systems and software designed for individual departments or functions can be adapted to create a world class manufacturing environment that's integrated companywide. Case studies reveal the common characteristics companies have shared in the challenge to computerize and provide guidelines for companies just starting out. This is a non-technical, practical guide.
ISBN 1-56327-046-3 / 424 pages / $50.00 / Order SOFT-B236

Performance Measurement for World Class Manufacturing
A Model for American Companies
Brian H. Maskell

If your company is adopting world class manufacturing techniques, you'll need new methods of performance measurement to control production variables. In practical terms, this book describes the new methods of performance measurement and how they are used in a changing environment. For manufacturing managers as well as cost accountants, it provides a theoretical foundation of these innovative methods supported by extensive practical examples. The book specifically addresses performance measures for delivery, process time, production flexibility, quality, and finance.
ISBN 0-915299-99-2 / 448 pages / $55.00 / Order PERFM-B236

Handbook for Productivity Measurement and Improvement
William F. Christopher and Carl G. Thor, eds.
An unparalleled resource! In over 100 chapters, nearly 80 front-runners in the quality movement reveal the evolving theory and specific practices of world-class organizations. Spanning a wide variety of industries and business sectors, they discuss quality and productivity in manufacturing, service industries, profit centers, administration, nonprofit and government institutions, health care and education. Contributors include Robert C. Camp, Peter F. Drucker, Jay W. Forrester, Joseph M. Juran, Robert S. Kaplan, John W. Kendrick, Yasuhiro Monden, and Lester C. Thurow. Comprehensive in scope and organized for easy reference, this compendium belongs in every company and academic institution concerned with business and industrial viability.
ISBN 1-56327-007-2 / 1344 pages / $90.00 / Order HPM-B236

Fast Focus on TQM
A Concise Guide to Companywide Learning
Derm Barrett
Finally, here's one source for all your TQM questions. Compiled in this concise, easy-to-read handbook are definitions and detailed explanations of over 160 key terms used in TQM. Organized in a simple alphabetical glossary form, the book can be used either as a primer for anyone being introduced to TQM or as a complete reference guide. It helps to align teams, departments, or entire organizations in a common understanding and use of TQM terminology. For anyone entering or currently involved in TQM, this is one resource you must have.
ISBN 1-56327-049-8 / 186 pages / $20.00 / Order FAST-B236

TO ORDER: Write, phone, or fax Productivity Press, Dept. BK, P.O. Box 13390, Portland, OR 97213-0390, phone 1-800-394-6868, fax 1-800-394- 6286. Send check or charge to your credit card (American Express, Visa, MasterCard accepted).

U.S. ORDERS: Add $5 shipping for first book, $2 each additional for UPS surface delivery. Add $5 for each AV program containing 1 or 2 tapes; add $12 for each AV program containing 3 or more tapes. We offer attractive quantity discounts for bulk purchases of individual titles; call for more information.

INTERNATIONAL ORDERS: Write, phone, or fax for quote and indicate shipping method desired. For international callers, telephone number is 503-235-0600 and fax number is 503-235-0909. Prepayment in U.S. dollars must accompany your order (checks must be drawn on U.S. banks). When quote is returned with payment, your order will be shipped promptly by the method requested.

NOTE: Prices are in U.S. dollars and are subject to change without notice.